HEADLINE ISSUES

Earth's Growing Population

Catherine Chambers

 Heinemann LIBRARY

www.heinemannlibrary.co.uk
Visit our website to find out more information about **Heinemann Library** books.

To order:
 Phone 44 (0) 1865 888066
 Send a fax to 44 (0) 1865 314091
 Visit the Heinemann Bookshop at www.heinemannlibrary.co.uk to browse our catalogue and order online.

Heinemann Library is an imprint of Capstone Global Library Limited, a company incorporated in England and Wales having its registered office at 7 Pilgrim Street, London, EC4V 6LB - Registered company number: 6695582

"Heinemann" is a registered trademark of Pearson Education Limited, under licence to Capstone Global Library Limited

Edited by Sarah Eason and Leon Gray
Designed by Calcium and Geoff Ward
Original illustrations © Capstone Global Library Limited 2009
Illustrated by Geoff Ward
Picture research by Maria Joannou
Originated by Heinemann Library
Printed and bound in China by CTPS

ISBN 978 0 431162 73 7 (hardback)
13 12 11 10 09
10 9 8 7 6 5 4 3 2 1

British Library Cataloguing in Publication Data
Chambers, Catherine, 1954-
   Earth's growing population. - (Headline issues)
   1. Population - Juvenile literature 2. Population policy
   - Juvenile literature
   I. Title
   363.9
A full catalogue record for this book is available from the British Library.

Acknowledgements
We would like to thank the following for permission to reproduce photographs:
Alamy Images: Neil Cooper 13r, Images of Africa Photobank 17t, Lou Linwei 21, Friedrich Stark 15; Corbis: Ammar Awad/Reuters 22, William Campbell/Sygma 5t, Ciro Fusco/EPA 13l, Bob Krist 5b, JP Laffont/Sygma 18, 19, Barry Lewis 29b, Pawel Libera 27t, Gideon Mendel 27b, Patrick Robert/Sygma 16, Peter Turnley 20; Dreamstime: Avlitrato 11t; FLPA: Nigel Cattlin 7; Fotolia: Bohanka 5, Denis Cordier 20–21, Alexey Klementiev 12–13; Getty Images: Paula Bronstein 25b, Per-Anders Pettersson 23; Istockphoto: Daniel Stein 17b, Peeter Viisimaa 18–19; Photolibrary Group 14; Rex Features: Sipa Press 9; Shutterstock: 3777190317 23, Andresr 14–15, Vera Bogaerts 24–25, Wong Kok Choy 6b, Dhoxax 8, 18, Christine F 6–7, Jorge R. Gonzalez 32, Jose Gil 16–17, Tatiana Grozetskaya 4, 32, Knotsmaster 16, Philip Lange 26–27, Rafael Ramirez Lee 29t, Kirsz Marcin 12, Girish Menon 8–9, Clara Natoli 11, Gijs van Ouwerkerk 28–29, Paulaphoto 20, Vishal Shah 8b, Perov Stanislav 14, Birute Vijeikiene 1, 24, Anthony Jay D. Villalon 10, Lisa F. Young 26, Khoo Eng Yow 7, A.S. Zain 3, 22; Still Pictures: Achim Pohl/Das Fotoarchiv 25t.

Cover photograph reproduced with permission of Getty Images/Lonely Planet Images/John Pennock.

Every effort has been made to contact copyright holders of material reproduced in this book. Any omissions will be rectified in subsequent printings if notice is given to the publishers.

12.99

Contents

Some words are printed in bold, **like this**. You can find out what they mean by looking in the glossary on page 30.

Population in the spotlight

According to the **United Nations** there are about 6.7 billion people living in the world today. However, the real figure is probably a lot higher than this, because it is very hard to count everybody very accurately. More importantly, the world's population is rising fast. By 2050, current estimates suggest that there will be more than nine billion people living on planet Earth.

Population problems

Some countries do not have enough resources to meet the needs of all their people. This means that many people go without food and water. They may live in cities with poor housing and **sanitation**. Children are not able to go to school, and there are few job opportunities.

Poor people cannot afford medical care when they are ill or energy for transport and heating.

Many of the world's **developing countries** cannot create enough wealth for their people. They do not have the resources, or political power within the world.

The wealthy world

Other countries can provide their people with most of the things that they need. The population may be small or there may be lots of jobs and access to education. Countries that can provide the right resources create wealth for their people. The people enjoy healthy and more prosperous lives. Most of these **developed countries** have a lot of political power in the world, too.

FACT!

The ten most populated countries in 2008 (numbers in brackets show population in millions) are:
✦ China (1325) ✦ India (1135) ✦ United States (305) ✦ Indonesia (231) ✦ Brazil (187)
✦ Pakistan (164) ✦ Bangladesh (159) ✦ Nigeria (148) ✦ Russia (142) ✦ Japan (128)

BEHIND THE
HEADLINES
Growing capital

People from all over Africa are flocking to Lagos – the capital of Nigeria – to find work. Lagos has become the fastest-growing and most heavily populated city in Africa. It is also one of the most expensive. The average Nigerian lives on less than $1 a day, while a box of cereal in Lagos costs $6.

These people are living in poverty in Lagos in Nigeria. They may have moved to the city to look for a job but, unable to get work, have found the cost of living to be very high.

More than 15.5 million people live in Shanghai, China, making this city one of the most heavily populated in the world.

Farming fails to feed the people

THERE IS ENOUGH food in the world to feed everyone. Some countries cannot feed their people, while in others people eat too much and are **obese**. The big issue is food distribution. The world's food does not always reach the people who need it most.

Farmers need a boost to grow food

There are at least 850 million people in the world who do not have enough to eat. This is partly because 80 per cent of farmers in **developing countries** have small plots of land and large families to feed. They have weak seed and poor storage for their **crops**.

Another problem occurs when developed countries sell cheap food **surpluses** to developing countries. This "**food dumping**" may solve food shortages in the short term, but it does not encourage farmers from the **developing world** to feed themselves **sustainably**.

Better together

Small farms in the developing world often face drought, plant diseases, and pests. Farmers are now forming groups called cooperatives. They share seeds, storage, and tools. They sell crops at local markets to earn cash. Some sell crops such as coffee to other countries. These activities help to feed and develop the local population.

Selling crops such as tea helps poorer countries to create much-needed income.

If the world shares its food we can end hunger: Who is right and who is wrong?

FOR

Some countries produce more food than they need. It is better for them to give it to countries that cannot feed their people than to see it go to waste.

So much surplus grain is grown in some countries that it is stockpiled in vast food mountains.

AGAINST

Sharing food is a short-term solution to a long-term problem. It is much better to help farmers to grow their own crops to provide food long into the future.

Cities bursting at the seams

MORE THAN HALF of all the people on the planet live in cities. Every day, about 180,000 people migrate from poor rural areas to cities to look for work. The cities are also centres of **commerce**, media, and the arts. They give people wider opportunities, but crowded cities put pressure on resources. Tough choices have to be made.

Many people are forced into even worse poverty when they move from rural areas to the city of Mumbai.

Planning nightmare for city populations

The Indian city of Mumbai is home to around 18 million people. More than half of all the people in the city live in poor houses with no **sanitation**. The city needs 84,000 new homes every year but only manages to build about 55,000. There are too many other pressures on public spending. One of these is for transport.

Progress through the railway

Mumbai is a huge centre for trade and business in India. The city needs better public transport to help drive the growing economy. The city has chosen to develop the rail network, which is used by more than six million people every day. New track is being laid. New railway carriages and engines have been ordered.

Thousands of people who live near the railway are being moved to make way for new track. Their homes are being bulldozed. A big rehousing project is planned, but it cannot keep apace with the people who need new city homes.

ON THE SPOT
Athens

Athens

Athens – the capital city of Greece – is home to 3.8 million people. However, there could be another two million **migrant workers** who live there, too. The rising population has seen an increase in traffic. **Pollution** has become a problem. Athens has reduced **emissions** using buses fuelled by natural gas, electric cars, and a bigger metro. Trees have been planted to absorb emissions.

Athens has tackled the problems of pollution by investing in the city's public transport system.

Water worries

At least 20 per cent of the Earth's growing population does not have access to clean drinking water. In unplanned areas of cities, called shanty towns or townships, people have to queue at temporary water pipes. In rural areas, people often have to walk to the nearest well, waterhole, or stream to get the water they need. The water supply can be miles from home. In some **developed countries**, water is used for leisure facilities such as swimming pools. This is causing water shortages.

Pollution in the water supply

Pollution from factories and industries such as mining reaches water supplies in many cities. Dangerous **pollutants** seep through the soil and poison underground water systems. Some of these pollutants are heavy metals such as mercury and lead, which damage peoples' nervous systems. In rural areas, farmers may use dangerous **pesticides** and **herbicides** that leak into village wells.

Wars over water

Water shortage is causing conflict between countries that share the same water supply. The situation will get worse as the world's population rises and the **climate** becomes drier. It has already caused problems between Turkey and its neighbours Iraq and Syria.

Syria's population is densely packed in the west of the country. This is because the harsh Syrian Desert lies to the east. Syria relies on Turkey to supply its water needs from the Euphrates River, which runs through both countries. In dry years, such as 2000, Turkey has not supplied enough. Syria blames the dams that Turkey has built along the Euphrates River.

Syria is now planning to divert trillions of litres of water from the Euphrates River before it flows downstream to Iraq. There is a chance that the entire region will break out into conflict in response to the water crisis.

BEHIND THE HEADLINES

Purifying water helps solve shortage

Nearly 98 per cent of the world's water is saltwater, which people cannot drink. Some dry countries, such as Australia, are building **desalination plants**. These make freshwater out of saltwater. Singapore recycles and purifies water for drinking. This is cheap and uses only one-third of the energy of the average desalination plant.

Some parts of Australia are desperately short of water. Desalination plants, such as the one above, may be the answer.

The Atatürk Dam generates electricity and provides water for the south-eastern Anatolia region of Turkey. Iraq and Syria may be suffering severe water shortages because of the dam.

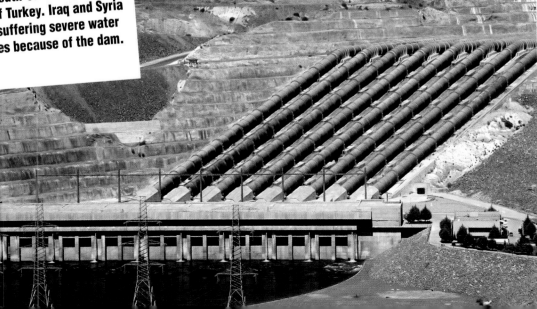

Sanitation and hygiene

POPULATION PRESSURE HAS led to stress on **sanitation** in both rural areas and the cities. Every year, about 60 million children are born into homes with no proper sanitation or running water. Poor sanitation and a lack of clean water cause illnesses such as **diarrhoea**, which leads to **dehydration**. This is the second-biggest killer of children under five years of age.

Raw sewage hits health

Open drains and raw **sewage** in unplanned city townships causes diseases such as typhoid. Poor people in rural areas cannot afford to build piped sewage systems on their small plots of land. Programmes to dig covered pit toilets in rural areas are a great success in many **developing countries**. However, there are not enough of these projects.

Naples hit by litter crisis

Crowded cities create huge amounts of litter. In 2008, the streets of Naples in Italy were lined with rubbish. All the landfill sites were full, and there was nowhere to put all the rubbish. Naples faced a litter crisis until Germany stepped in to help and agreed to take the rubbish away.

Disease looms near litter mountains

With litter comes disease, pests, and poisons. Burning litter creates **toxic** fumes, so in many countries the litter is left to build up into huge mountains. Many people in the developing world make their homes next to the litter mountains. Searching the litter for scrap to sell is the only way these people can earn a living.

FACT!

✦ Every minute seven children around the world die of diarrhoea caused by poor-quality drinking water and malnutrition.

✦ 80 per cent of the British population lives within 2 kilometres (1.25 miles) of a landfill site.

ON THE SPOT
Addis Ababa

Addis Ababa is the crowded capital city of Ethiopia. New sanitation blocks are being built in overcrowded townships. The blocks include taps, toilets, showers, and washing areas for clothes. The blocks have improved the health of the local people. They have also enabled women to spend more time working and less time walking miles to fetch water.

Yemen

Addis Ababa

Somalia

Ethiopia

Litter lines the streets of Naples in Italy, creating a health hazard.

These Ethiopian people are working together to build a sanitation block in Addis Ababa.

Housing hits the headlines

ACROSS THE WORLD, around 600 million people from cramped urban areas live in poor-quality houses. In rural areas, where many people have lots of children, more than one billion people live in overcrowded housing. Poor living conditions cause diseases such as bronchitis, **diarrhoea**, and mental problems. Poor and overcrowded housing brings social problems such as crime, especially among the young. In the developed world, housing is expensive and uses up a lot of the money people earn, leaving little for necessities such as food and warmth.

Housing at crisis point

On average, there are about six or seven people living in every township house in the developing world. Most of these houses have just one room. People build rough shelters using aluminium sheeting, plastic, and cardboard. They live in broken-down buses. In rural areas, large families do not have enough money to maintain their homes. They do not have enough land to build new homes for their children.

New ways for housing

Straw bales, reinforced canvas, stone rubble, clay, and kit frames made from renewable wood are all being used to help solve the housing problem. New designs are saving space and materials on a public housing project in Jaunapur, India. Domed roofs built from brick are strong but do not need steel supports. Recycled stone rubble is used to infill the brick circles.

High-rise flats dominate the skyline of Bogotá in Colombia. Poor neighbourhoods are found in the southern part of the city.

ON THE SPOT
Mathare, Kenya

Mathare is a sprawling township on the edge of Nairobi, Kenya. It is home to 500,000 people who all live in poor housing conditions. The Mathare Roots Youth Group brings young people together through education, technology, skills, and sport. The group helps to stop crime and open up opportunities. Its slogan is "From Roots to Fruits".

Uganda

Somalia

Kenya

Nairobi

Tanzania

Indian Ocean

Many Kenyan people live in townships like Mathare on the outskirts of Nairobi.

People put a strain on power

ENERGY IS A big issue for the world's growing population. China now uses more energy than any other nation. The United States uses more per person than anywhere else on Earth. By 2030, Brazil, China, and India will double their energy needs as their population and economies grow.

People without power

The world's population is growing, but energy resources are not. Fuels such as oil and natural gas are harder to find and more expensive to extract. In 2008, the price of **fossil fuels** increased and led to higher costs of food production. Food prices soared and riots started in many different countries around the world.

Power or pollution?

People are polluting the world with car fumes. They are using too much energy to heat their homes. A blanket of **carbon gases** in the **atmosphere** is heating the planet and causing **climate change**. This will continue as the world's population continues to grow.

Powerful ways

Wind and solar power could be the energy solutions for the future. Using less energy is the best solution of all. Housing experiments in densely populated cities use very little or no energy. The Sun heats homes through thick glass sheets. Solar panels provide hot water. Walls and roofs are insulated. Rotating chimneys suck in clean air and get rid of the stale air.

People protest on the streets of Algiers in Algeria. They are complaining about the rising cost of food and rising unemployment.

BEHIND THE HEADLINES

Solar stoves save trees

Collecting firewood in rural parts of the world is becoming harder and more time-consuming. Burning wood is not sustainable for the land or energy needs. Charcoal-burning stoves and solar stoves are being used in countries such as Bolivia, Kenya, Somalia, and Sudan. Solar stoves save about 30 per cent of wood.

Solar-powered stoves use the heat from the Sun to cook food.

Los Angeles, USA, suffers from air **pollution** in the form of smog, which is the result of **emissions** from vehicles.

Population pressure hits jobs hard

TOWNS AND CITIES are full of people looking for job opportunities. In many **developing countries**, people often come from rural areas where there may be no way for them to earn any money. This movement of people to city centres is called an "off-the-map" population. No one provides training and opportunities for this hidden work force. They will take whatever work they can.

This child is selling sweets in a Turkish port. Like many children from poor families in Asia, he must work to help support his family.

Children pay the price

More than 246 million children around the world are forced to work to support their families. Around 70 per cent of these child workers take jobs in rural areas. They often work in dusty mines and quarries. Some work for 12 hours a day on large **industrial farms**. They may be exposed to dangerous **pesticides** and **herbicides**. In the cities, children work in crowded backstreet factories. Some work as cleaners, while others sell goods on the streets.

Stopping the rush from rural areas

Many governments and aid organizations are trying to create more wealth in rural areas. They hope it will stop people from moving to overcrowded cities. It may also help families to cope without forcing their children into work. In some countries, small bank loans called **microcredit** agreements and basic financial advice are helping families in rural areas set up small businesses. Cooperatives and Fairtrade organizations help farmers to sell **surplus crops** and set up small factories.

ON THE SPOT
Philippines

Children seen working or begging on the streets of Philippine towns and cities are known as "street children". There are about 1.5 million children currently working on the streets. Some 75 per cent of these children do not live on the streets. They go home at the end of each working day to families who depend on their earnings to survive. These children are the lucky ones. The remaining 25 per cent of street children are homeless. They suffer many problems as a result of their living conditions, including ill health and physical abuse or violence.

Children as young as three are regularly seen working on the Philippine streets. This young girl is selling fruit from a street stall.

Poor health care for many people

THE WORLD'S POOREST people worry about losing their families to disease, so they have more children just in case. The overcrowding then adds to the world's health problems. This cycle is very hard to break.

Population and disease

In the developing world, many people die of infectious diseases such as **malaria** and **tuberculosis**. However, most people in overpopulated areas die of **pneumonia**. Poor heating and ventilation in bad housing are partly to blame. All these diseases are preventable and curable, but they are made worse by overcrowding.

Floods and disease

Natural disasters, especially floods, hit the health of people in overpopulated countries such as Bangladesh. Annual flood waters bring sewage to the surface, which causes diseases such as **cholera** and **dysentery**. During the floods, the government gives out clean water to protect flood victims from disease.

Long stainless steel **tube wells** are put inside normal wells. They reach far down in the ground to bring up clean water for people.

Medical bills hit large families

Poor people often cannot afford the health care that they need. In rural India, large families are struggling to cope with medical bills. Farmers may have to sell their land to pay the bills. Their children might have to work to help pay the debts and feed the family.

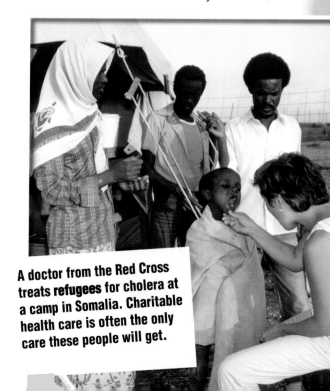

A doctor from the Red Cross treats refugees for cholera at a camp in Somalia. Charitable health care is often the only care these people will get.

A one-child policy will control population growth: Who is right and who is wrong?

FOR

It is irresponsible of parents to have more than one child when there are already too many people on the planet. How will we feed everyone? Where will they live?

These school children have no brothers or sisters. The government in China allows parents to have just one child.

AGAINST

It is up to the parents to decide how many children they should have. Governments should not be allowed to interfere with personal decisions such as these.

War devastates Earth's population

War and conflict force people to flee from their homes to neighbouring countries. The **refugees** put the existing population under pressure. There are at least 35 million refugees in the world today.

The Al Tanf refugee camp for homeless Palestinians lies between Iraq and Syria.

People fleeing to crowded camps

War hits rural areas hard. In war zones, restricted movement affects **livestock** farming. Herders cannot take their livestock to the best pastures. People cannot grow **crops** for fear of attack. They become poor and are forced to sell their land and livestock. Many end up in refugee camps where there are pressures on food and water.

Refugees put pressure on employment

There are very few jobs for refugees. Countries such as Lebanon in the Middle East are home to thousands of Palestinian refugees. Lebanon does not have enough work for its own people. So the Lebanese government stops the refugees from getting work. The Palestinians can only take part in market trading and services such as tailoring.

FACT!
- In 2000, the largest refugee group in the world was the Palestinians.
- Sudan holds 4.5 million refugees – more than any other country in the world (as of 2008).

BEHIND THE HEADLINES
Zimbabwe

Zimbabwe in Central Africa was once a thriving nation that grew all its own food. It is now torn by political fighting. At least three million refugees have fled to nearby South Africa. South Africa is the richest African nation. However, nearly half of its people have no work. Huge townships battle for resources. In 2008, some South Africans attacked refugees from Zimbabwe.

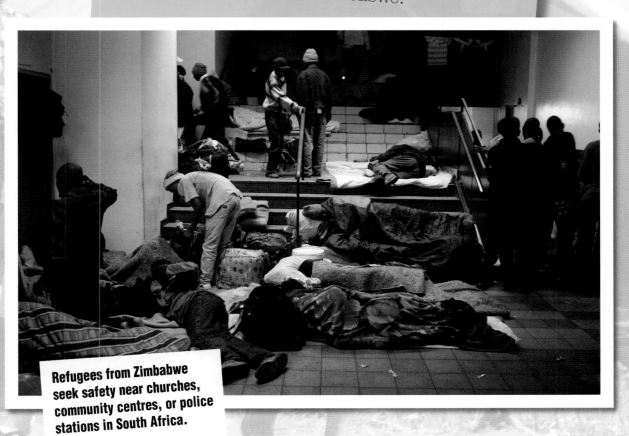

Refugees from Zimbabwe seek safety near churches, community centres, or police stations in South Africa.

Education for a stable population

ONE OF THE best ways to reduce the problems often associated with overpopulation is to educate people, but this is not always easy. Most **developing countries** with large populations find it hard to provide education for everyone.

Adult education reduces overpopulation

Education helps parents give their families a better standard of living. Children have a greater chance of good health. Parents have fewer children because their existing ones will survive.

Education works in two ways. It gives people the chance to get a good job. It also helps people to create wealth through business. Educated people no longer depend on food grown on overworked plots of land. They can earn much more than just a few pence a day.

Educated women

Women use their education to learn how to look after their children. Just two years of primary education will reduce the chances of infant death. The parents are confident that their children will survive. They are keen to give these children an education, too.

Business and education

Many educated women set up small businesses. They use the extra money to educate their children. These women aim to raise a small, educated family rather than a large family with poor skills. However, many girls still spend time doing household chores, such as fetching freshwater, when they could be going to school. Indeed, 11 per cent more girls in developing countries would attend school if there was freshwater close to their homes.

An adult education class in La Paz, Bolivia, helps people learn to read and write.

ON THE SPOT
Thailand

The education of girls has been a priority in Thailand in South-east Asia for decades. This has led the population growth to fall from 3.1 per cent in 1960 to 0.64 per cent in 2008. The greatest challenge the country now faces is raising awareness of diseases such as human immunodeficiency virus (**HIV**).

Both boys and girls now receive an education in Thailand.

Nations need more people

WHILE THE POPULATION of many countries is spiralling out of control, some countries face a completely different population problem – not enough people!

According to the **United Nations**, around 75 per cent of the **developed countries** will not have enough people by 2050. Even today, some countries do not have enough people. Some do not have enough young people to do different types of jobs or pay taxes. The taxes go toward services such as hospitals, schools, transport systems, and the emergency services. They also pay for pensions. These are payments given to people to help them when they are older.

Standard of living

Since World War II, many parents in Europe have had only one child – or maybe two. Many smaller families enjoyed a higher standard of living than some of the bigger families. Parents could afford to give their children a better education and more opportunities. However, now there are not enough people at work to pay tax to run the country.

Poor health causes population decline

In some countries, poor health care is destroying populations. People are dying much younger. The governments of many Eastern European countries do not support health care, so people are not living to old age. In Africa, the biggest problem is **HIV**/AIDS (Acquired Immunodeficiency Syndrome). In 2007, the United Nations estimated that more than 33 million people in the world had HIV. More than 22 million of these people were living in sub-Saharan Africa.

FACT!

Some populations in steady decline and the reasons behind it (population given in millions):
- ◆ Belarus (9.7) low birth rate and earlier deaths
- ◆ Czech Republic (10.4) low birth rate
- ◆ Germany (82.2) low birth rate
- ◆ Botswana (1.9) HIV/AIDS
- ◆ Swaziland (1.1) HIV/AIDS

BEHIND THE HEADLINES
Workers from other lands

Many European nations have tried to persuade people to have more children by offering financial incentives and good nursery care. This has not been enough. So they have encouraged **immigration**. Many people have come from Africa. Their cultures have added to city life.

Many African people make up a large part of the work force in western countries.

People from many African countries are dying from the HIV/AIDS epidemic.

Get involved!

By 2050 there will be more than nine billion people living in the world. Many charities and aid organizations see this as a crisis for the future.

In China, the word *crisis* is written with two characters. One means "danger" and the other means "opportunity". The dangers of overpopulation to the planet are clear, but there are opportunities, too. We are turning to new technologies to provide enough food, shelter, water, and energy without harming our precious planet. We can all get involved to make this happen.

Overpopulation causes environmental damage

Many people think that the world's growing population is responsible for destroying the environment. In some parts of Africa, farmers engage in slash-and-burn agriculture. They clear the forest to get more land. They use the land to grow **crops** to feed their families and earn money.

When all the nutrients in the soil have been used up, the farmers move on to new areas of forest and repeat the process. Vast areas of rainforest have been destroyed by slash-and-burn agriculture. New food technologies and a sustainable water source could help them reduce their land consumption. To help, everyone can support aid organizations that offer technological assistance.

Profit not overpopulation

In parts of Asia and South America, the forests are being cleared for farms and industries such as mining and logging. These industries make huge profits for big businesses, but they put very little money back to support the local populations.

Most of the wild prairies of the United States have been cleared for industrial agriculture. This type of farming uses modern farming methods to grow as much food as possible. Crops are sold in order to make a profit, rather than just provide food for local people.

A workers' cooperative in the Chiapas region of Mexico make and sell this colourful fabric.

THINGS TO DO

- Support farming and craft cooperatives such as Fairtrade. They help to support and bring wealth to rural communities.

- Go Green! The world's population is using up precious natural resources. It is polluting the air, land, and waters. We can all help through recycling and buying biodegradable products.

- Support a water-aid charity. These charities help to supply a sustainable water source, which is good for the environment. They help provide ecofriendly solutions to **sanitation**, too.

The Samburu people from Kenya live off their **livestock**, which can provide for almost all their needs.

Glossary

atmosphere layer of air that surrounds the Earth

carbon gas gas produced by cars and factories when they burn fossil fuels

cholera disease carried in polluted water. It affects the digestive system.

climate types of weather that usually occur in a place at different times of the year

climate change unexpected changes to the weather caused by global warming

commerce trade and business services

crops plants grown by farmers

dehydration the loss of too much fluid from the body

desalination plant factory where salt is removed from seawater to provide water to drink

developed country rich country

developing country poor country

diarrhoea stomach upset that leads to a dangerous loss of fluid

dysentery disease carried in polluted water. Dysentery causes diarrhoea and abdominal pain.

emission gases and drops of liquid let out from exhausts or chimneys

food dumping when rich nations dump cheap food onto poorer nations

fossil fuel fuel such as coal, oil, and natural gas

herbicide chemical used to kill weeds among crops

HIV virus that breaks down the body's immune system and may lead to a serious disease called AIDS

immigration when people come from another country to live and work

industrial farms farming on a large scale, using chemicals and big machinery to maximise profit

livestock animals used for meat and milk, such as sheep, goats and cattle

malaria infectious disease caused by tiny germs that are spread through the bites of some types of mosquitoes

microcredit small loans to set up businesses or pay for training

migrant worker person who is born in one country and works in another

obese being excessively overweight

pesticide substance sprayed over crops to kill pests such as insects

pneumonia infection of the lungs

pollutant any substance that causes pollution

pollution harm to the environment caused by poisonous chemicals

refugee person who is forced out of his or her country

sanitation drainage systems for dealing with sewage

sewage waste materials such as human waste

surplus more goods than are needed

sustainably way of doing something that can be continued for a long time

toxic poisonous

tuberculosis disease caused by a germ that usually attacks the lungs

tube well steel tube pushed deep down to draw up clean water

United Nations international organization that tries to protect human rights, end poverty, fight disease, and prevent war

Find out more

Books

Can Earth Support Our Growing Population? (What Do You Think?),
Kate Shuster (Heinemann, 2008)

Graphing Population (Real World Data), Isabel Thomas
(Heinemann, 2009)

Population (Planet Under Pressure), Paul Mason (Heinemann, 2007)

Population Explosion (Can the Earth Cope?), Ewan McLeish (Hodder
Wayland, 2008)

Population Growth (Earth's Changing Landscape), Philip Steele
(Franklin Watts Ltd, 2007)

Population Growth (Sustaining Our Environment), Rufus Bellamy
(Franklin Watts Ltd, 2009)

Websites

Children in Crisis is an organization that aims to give children from
poor countries the educational opportunities they need to help
transform their lives. Find out more at:
www.childrenincrisis.org/

This fun website includes lots of information to help children help
the environment:
www.kidsforsavingearth.org

This website is run by the charity Planet 21. It looks at some of the
key issues that face the world's population, such as famine, health,
pollution, and poverty, and tells you what you can do to help:
www.peopleandplanet.net/

Unicef is the largest global organization working especially for
children. Check out the "Voices of Youth" link to find out more
information about the issues that really matter at:
www.unicef.org/voy/

Index